BE YOUR WHOLE SELF:

Where self-help fails and what you can do about it.

Dionne Kasian-Lew

Publication date: March 2013

Published by: Dugdale-Woolf Publishing

Version 1.0 © Dionne Kasian-Lew 2013

Table of Contents

Nurturing

Introduction

What You Can Expect

Be Your Whole Self:

1. Provides insights on where some self-help fails;

2. Looks at what we mean by being who we are, why we disconnect and how we can move towards being whole;

3. Gives you three powerful exercises that practiced regularly will clear emotional blocks and build your energy; and

4. Invites you to adopt a daily practice based on mindfulness, self-honesty and kindness.

This book is designed to fit into your busy daily life. The exercises, although seemingly simple, require commitment and courage to practice. Mindful tasks performed daily, over a lifetime, define your life.

About Me

If you have been drawn to *Be Your Whole Self* then I am going to guess that you are already a long way down your path. You were probably asking 'Who am I?' and 'Why am I here?' even before you skipped into kindergarten. I bet you have been chasing those answers, in some way or another, your whole life.

I also imagine that life has blessed you with enough difficulties to make you wonder if it was worth the search. Was your father a drunk? Did you have a domineering mother or one that abandoned you? Did you open your eyes and find you were hanging on to life by a thread, feeling that the last time you looked, you were flying out of control down the hill on your bike?

Life is filled with all sorts of experiences and pretty much any of us can take the good with the bad. But if the bad starts to overtake the good, if nothing we do is right or enough, if we are so hurt that being alive is always painful, then we struggle.

Sometimes, a single trauma outside anyone's control has such a strong impact that we feel we can't go beyond it.

And so we leave. Not literally of course. To all intents and purposes we are still walking around. But we split, withdrawing our wounded spirits from our bodies. The body becomes like an empty vessel, unconnected to our thoughts. And as for our feelings, we freeze them out.

But wait a minute – didn't you say you wanted to know who you were?

Did you think you could work it out in your head? Or find a panacea you could pop into your mouth like a pill? Did you think, like I used to, that if you read enough or talked enough the answers would all appear? What was your holy grail - money, Buddhism, other people? Are your shelves heaving under the weight of books you thought would bring that elusive prize – self-knowing, great relationships, purposeful work, or physical and financial health? And did you find that no matter how much you learned you could not shake the patterns that caused you the deepest pain, those that continued to hold you back, no matter how much progress you made in other areas?

Ever found yourself thinking: *Oh no, not this again?*

Maybe you're financially secure and happily married, but you still worry about what everyone thinks about you. Or you can't keep a relationship, or a job? Or is yours the subtler but no less soul-wrenching variety; you look like the 'whole package' on the outside but you're not really authentic. You are appropriate perhaps, but not real?

Repeat these patterns enough and you might start wondering if there is something more to them than meets the eye. I did.

What I found was that these patterns were underpinned by fears that caused me to behave in certain ways.

The fears had developed over the course of my life so that certain events triggered feelings that I found uncomfortable. This set-up distorted my belief systems, for example, if I was not perfect then I didn't deserve love. You will have your own version.

For a long time it was easier for me to avoid discomfort by using familiar exit strategies, but that only reinforced my patterns. After that happened enough, it dawned on me that by learning to sit in discomfort, to accept what I was feeling and be present, I could choose a different response.

I was initially disappointed to find that there were no answers 'outside', waiting to be found. I think many of us crave this way out. We think a new person or philosophy will fill the gaps.

But the answers are in the patterns themselves.

The patterns reveal the beliefs that trigger you. Your job is to find ways to observe, accept and embrace them.

The saving grace of this process, although it can be uncomfortable, is that the decision-making power about how you behave, the thing that pretty much defines who you are, rests with you. You don't have to wait for the right person, philosophy or time to save you. But you do need the tools.

So you too must have asked the question. And you got the answer - you got what you needed to work with your holy grail experientially: *your life*.

This book is my attempt to articulate some of the processes I uncovered while closing my own gaps; to share tools I discovered that moved me from feeling victimised and valueless to living consciously, responsibly, compassionately, and with a sense of worth and an acceptance of my flaws, most of the time.

You may not have pulled all the parts together, but I'll bet you have most of the pieces in the palm of your hand. There may be gaps. I hope *Be Your Whole Self* can help you identify where they are. Usually they are those places you dare not tread. Many healers say we avoid dealing with our blocks because we are scared. That might be true, but just as often we don't know what tools to use.

There are many paths to self-understanding. This is just one way and if it doesn't resonate for you, I encourage you to try other options.

Be Your Whole Self explains why I believe that reading or talking, the cornerstone of many self-help practices, is not enough and that real growth results from seeking to learn, paying attention, being willing to sit in discomfort, creatively expressing yourself in whatever area appeals to you (for example, stockbroking, cooking, painting) and understanding that there is no cut-and-dried answer to life.

I encourage you to question the platitudes that you have been fed about what it means to be valuable or spiritual; to decide for yourself, including of course thinking about anything that I say that does not sit well with you.

Who Would Benefit?

If you feel like you're living in your head and not your body, then you will benefit from some of the practices in *Be Your Whole Self.*

If you've been hurt and you want to get beyond that, but you don't know how to shift all the resentments that you are carrying, then you will benefit from *Be Your Whole Self.*

If you've noticed that the same destructive patterns repeat over and over again, no matter what you do and you want to change that, then you will benefit from *Be Your Whole Self.*

If you feel like one part of yourself had developed out of balance with the others, if you're intellectually bright but emotionally stunted, or emotionally aware but mentally unclear, or physically fit but spiritually closed, or spiritually aware but unhealthy and unfit, *Be Your Whole Self* can help bring you back to balance.

In other words, if you're the kind of person who longs to live a purposeful life, then *Be Your Whole Self* could help. You already know that 'just surviving' is not enough. You need more than just a great job, financial security, even a wonderful relationship – not because you are greedy – but because you need to know who you are and why you are here. Nothing stops this longing, not even you.

Being sensitive in this world is hard, because we feel everything so deeply. As a result many of us get hurt and shut down. We develop all sorts of defences to shield ourselves from the world. We believe the things we are told about ourselves and take them on board (into our bodies) as if they were the truth. Over time we become confused by others' interpretations of who we are or should be.

Be Your Whole Self is about remembering who you are and creating who you want to be. It's not about mindless affirmations or the kind of quick-fix thinking that leaves people more disconnected because they deny reality. These techniques help you to go into the discomfort you have previously avoided, the pain that keeps the masks in place and transforms you at the core.

What you will find as you embody this is that your sensitivity will help you develop your gifts. It gives you the qualities you need to live purposefully and according to your values.

We who seek to be our whole selves know that there is more to life than what appears on the surface. No matter what we achieve, we long to experience a deeper connection. And we read, we talk, we move, we do whatever we can to create it.

Where Self-Help Fails

Many people long to heal and are willing to do the hard work but a lot of the techniques they try fail them. There are many reasons for that.

You cannot heal in your head – you need to heal in your body.

A lot of self-help techniques are superficial. Many focus on changing the way people think. While there is no doubt what you think impacts on your life, you cannot heal in your head.

There is a reason you have a body. There is a reason you feel, and there is a reason you dream. These all function together. You have to grow on every level if you want to be whole.

Trying to heal your thoughts without also learning to be emotionally present is like trying to fix the roof on a house without walls. No matter how hard you try, the rain and wind will still get in.

I am not a fan of positive thinking, but even for those who are, the problem is that many commit to it for a few minutes a day. The rest of the time they return to their familiar patterns. No wonder they don't manifest their desires overnight. That's a bit like eating a banana and muesli for breakfast, then stuffing your face with fizzy drinks and fries for every other meal and wondering why you don't lose weight.

I also think it's difficult to teach people to control their thoughts. *Don't think of a white elephant* is a classic technique that demonstrates the complexity of trying not to think in certain ways. It's far more powerful to be aware of what you are thinking and the feelings that those thoughts trigger, and then start to make decisions about how you will respond to these.

You cannot rise above your emotions – you need to go into and through them to transform

There's also a lot of misunderstanding about what our emotions are and how we should deal with them.

We often divide emotions into good and bad emotions and try to stop ourselves feeling the 'bad' ones.

Don't get me wrong; we do it with the best of intentions. We all want to be good people. But by denying what we feel, we remain disconnected. It's okay to be angry. And if you let yourself be angry when it's appropriate then the anger is not going to build up. But if you try to tell yourself that being angry is bad and you respond to someone slapping you in the face with a smile, then not only do you send the wrong message about how much you value yourself, but also your anger goes underground. It's like a pressure cooker. One day it bursts. Someone stamps on your foot by accident and they get the brunt of 30 years of pent-up rage that has nothing to do with them.

When you learn that it's safe to feel anything – from joy to pain to anger to frustration to freedom – then you don't fear your emotions any more. You allow yourself to have them. You know whatever you are feeling will transform into something else in good time.

At the start of a healing journey, most people are in denial about the level of pain, anger and hurt they feel.

Most of us skate on the surface of consciousness because we are so afraid of what will happen if we stand still and actually experience the emotions we are carrying. One of the most powerful techniques you can ever develop is the ability to be present through any emotion you are experiencing. Once you can do this, you can do almost anything.

Wounds are not the enemy that needs to be destroyed – they are gifts that need to be understood

Many techniques refer to people's wounds as if they were cancers to be annihilated – the chemotherapy of choice of course being *change your thinking*.

But our wounds need to be understood. They are maps that mark a path from our defended self back to the connected self. They can appear as addictions or destructive behaviours and they carry important information about what we need to learn. We don't get rid of a wound. We examine it, understand it, experience it and transform it.

Blaming makes us victims – we need to accept responsibility as adults for becoming whole

Greater than all of these failings, in my view, is that some self-help theories keep people feeling victimised because they do not challenge the people to take responsibility for their lives.

We become adults when we accept responsibility for our lives. I am not saying we are responsible for everything that has been done to us. But we are responsible for how we behave in response to it. This is not always easy.

We are responsible for facing our darkness, for recognising that the things we feel most victimised about are things we have done ourselves. I am not saying that if you were abused, you went on to abuse someone else, not at all. I am saying that if for example someone stepped over your boundaries, and then you look at your life, you will discover a time that you have done exactly that, if not to someone else, then to yourself.

If you are willing to look at yourself clearly, you will discover that these key patterns manifest in different ways throughout your life. Without even meaning to, we sometimes choose people or situations that allow us to recreate the experience. Unconsciously this reinforces our belief that this is the way life works.

This deep, dark world, this painful recognition that we betray ourselves as much as those who have betrayed us, is so freeing.

We no longer hate ourselves for being imperfect. We drop our resentments. We stop blaming everyone else for what they have done to us and look at what we have done to ourselves, not to judge, but to bring about our healing.

No matter how good your personal trainer you cannot get or stay fit in a single session – true change is a lifelong practice

And last, but not least, the key reason why most healing fails is because it does not become a daily practice.

Sometimes we work through a certain process that is very powerful and revealing. We learn a lot and move on to the next thing.

But healing cannot be accomplished in one session in the same way that you cannot get fit in one session, even if you have the best personal trainer in the world.

A personal trainer can guide you to the exercises you need to get the most reward for your effort. But you have got to show up – day in and day out.

Becoming whole is no different.

Be Your Whole Self is based on simple but effective tools that require ongoing practice. If you do them, you will reap the benefits. And, like a fitness program, some of those benefits will be immediate but the real and lasting change – the reshaping – will come over time.

It's up to you. No one can take your journey for you.

In summary, often we fail to achieve lasting healing because:

1. We try to think ourselves into wholeness;

2. We deny the depth and breadth of our emotions;

3. We avoid or try to get rid of our emotional wounds;

4. We blame others rather than taking responsibility; and

5. We do not commit to nurturing as a daily practice.

Be Your Whole Self is based on techniques that:

1. Shifts healing from just thinking about it to doing it;

2. Teaches us to respect all our emotions;

3. Helps us how to understand the gifts in our wounds;

4. Encourages us to take responsibility for our behaviour; and

5. Reinforces the need for daily practice.

The Practice

Becoming whole is a lot like becoming fit, it's something you have to do.

You can't get there by reading a book, in the same way that you can't get fit by buying a gym membership. That is why this book includes tools that require daily practice.

As part of the process I will ask you to assess where you are and how you got there. Stocktaking is important because it allows you to deal with your life realistically and work out why things are the way they are. There is always a chain of cause and effect.

Next, you need to articulate where you want to go.

Clearly, to extend the analogy, someone who wants to become a long distance runner is going to need a different set of exercises from the one who wants to become a bodybuilding champion, and the same applies to personal goals.

Knowing what you want allows you to work out when you have achieved it. Of course, if along the way you change your mind, that's fine. Goals do shift, but we can only know this if we have something to change in the first place.

Once you know where you are heading, more or less, the book provides some insights that will hopefully help you to get there. In a fitness program, this might be the equivalent of understanding the relationship between food and fat, knowing how to monitor your heart rate to achieve the maximum benefits from the work you are doing or being given warm up, stretching and building exercises for all the different sets of muscles in the body. The basic information is the same for everyone, even though the way you use it will vary.

Once we know the routine, the key is practice. Practice not only strengthens us to move up to the next level, it also reveals where we are out of alignment and may need additional work. Eventually we reassess and refine our process, setting new goals and varying what we have learned. The cycle becomes a way of life, as natural as breathing.

Being Who We Are

Who Are We And Can We Not Be Who We Are

Many of us are disembodied or split, what we think of as out of sync with what we feel and do.

For example, we may say we're happy when we're not really but we think we should be. Or we deny that we're angry because we have the misguided idea it's not right or spiritual. Or we pretend to be less capable than we are because we need to prop up someone else's ego. The list goes on.

There are many reasons we do that from the way we've been socialised to the expectations of our culture. Another key influence is that we've been taught to value our intellect above our emotions, and that the mind can and should control what we feel. And while being mindful is an important component of self-growth, it is really not that simple.

To be whole means to express all of our emotions. I don't mean in an undisciplined way but in a way that is real and respectful. This is much harder in practice than theory, because while it's easy to be happy, we don't tend to deal well with discomfort. A 'negative' thought emerges and we tell ourselves: *I should not be angry/sad/frustrated* – substituting that feeling for something more palatable. We think this makes us good, but what it really makes us is inauthentic, half people.

Of the many myths about emotional life, I think one of the worst is that it can be divided into good and bad. This puts an invisible pressure on us to split, expressing only a single, sanctioned side of who we are.

But our dark feelings don't go away. They move underground where they tend to fester until one day they burst out, often in destructive ways. Writers like Johnson and Ruhl refer to these rejected parts of ourselves as the 'Unlived Life' and believe that they must be brought to light if we are to have a meaningful existence.

To be fully human is to navigate the depth and breadth of feeling. And although there's no doubt that having a positive mindset can be helpful, there's something grotesque about stretching ourselves across the rack of *positive, positive, positive* all the time. It's exhausting!

Life is flux. We breathe in, we breathe out, one without the other and we die. Love is natural, but so is frustration and despair, and we need to accept that all are part of being alive.

Professor Seligman, founder of the positive psychology movement, distinguished an engaged and meaningful life from the transience of pure pleasure seeking. That is not the same as being happy all of the time.

The Buddhists teach us not to attach to our emotions and this means to accept them without craving or resistance. It does not mean, as people often misinterpret it, that we should not feel them or vague them out. This only reinforces denial.

Instead, attachment arises when we attribute the source of our feelings to something outside of ourselves and so focus on it inappropriately. For example in a relationship, we assume it is our partner who makes us happy/sad and so we make them responsible for how we feel, asking them to be what we want them to be, rather than loving them for who they really are. We need to learn how to allow each emotion its place and find a way of expressing it that does not harm others or ourselves. This is not easy. Faced with difficulty, most of us reach for an addiction or lash out as a way of deflecting ourselves from the pain.

It's also important to avoid self-indulgence by just expressing our emotions without using them as an opportunity to understand the underlying issue. Ask yourself: *Why am I feeling this way?* You will gain important insights about your own process.

How do you label your feelings? Do you divide them into good or bad, the either/or that does not allow for ambiguity? Are only certain feelings legitimate? Becoming aware of what you believe about the emotional life, and why, is the first step to freeing yourself from the limitations of living an emotional half-life and moves you one step further on the path towards being authentic.

Why do we develop emotional blockages?

Our basic response to pain is to contract and so we become less and less of who we are (yes, I know that defining that is difficult) as we face life's difficulties.

When we are young, we don't know how to deal with pain so we cut off. Our wounds are like splinters that are too painful to dig out and so we adjust the way we behave instead. Imagine if you spent your life walking on the ball of your foot to avoid a splinter in your heel. Eventually you would throw your ankles and hips and even your back out of joint.

Emotionally it works the same way. When we avoid a part of ourselves, we set up ways of behaving that may numb the pain but which throw the other parts out of whack. These are called defences. By the time we are adults, we are so used to our defences that we often mistake them for who we are.

To get back in touch with our emotions we need to move through the layers of protection and deal with the original issue. One change triggers another and over time all the parts of our lives come back into alignment.

We can stay blocked because we don't know how to handle the discomfort that arises when we look at the block. Sometimes it challenges our idea of who we are.

Who we are is complex. It changes over time. There is no fixed and immutable self but there is an aware and authentic self, lived consistent with our values. That means knowing first what your values are, and which are yours and which belong to someone else.

Can You Not Be Who You Are?

An obvious question for anyone on a journey towards 'being who you really are' is: *Can you be anything else?* This depends on what you believe the self is. There is no easy answer, the question having been asked and answered differently since the beginning of time.

Are you a product of genetics, environment or both? Do you have a core, or is character fluid? Do things have an inherent existence, or, as the Buddhists argue, is meaning always dependent on (or caused by) something else?

While I can't know, I will add that being who we are (whatever that is) consciously – rather than unconsciously – matters. The unexamined life, as Socrates said, is not worth living. And in order to examine our lives, we need to start asking questions.

Even before we're born we are picking up cues. We role model our families and absorb languages and cultural norms. This is the marvel of the human brain but also its shortcoming. We can go from the womb to adulthood without any idea of what drives us.

We can confuse this collage of absorbed phenomena with a self. But once we start probing beneath the surface, we see that unknown forces largely drive us. Those seeking self-awareness want to know what those forces are. This is the 'reality' of being

31

who you are - the mindful understanding of your self, not as something perfect or permanent, but as something that was created and can be <u>recreated</u>. But you need to know what made it up in the first place.

A thinking person draws widely on the information around them and within them, synthesising it, forming an independent point of view complete with the recognition: *I could be wrong.* The outcome is less important that asking the questions.

We Are Born Whole But Unaware

We are born whole. As children, we love being in our bodies, we are connected to nature and we allow ourselves to think or feel or say whatever comes up without trying to manage it. We know ourselves so well that we don't even think about self-knowing.

It's only as we get older that we start to separate out 'acceptable' and 'not acceptable' parts.

This is in part due to socialisation, which is understandable. We are part of a broader social structure that requires rules. And some rules are fine, but they can be damaging if they are highly restrictive or deliberately hurtful.

Becoming adult is neither about total acceptance, nor outright rebellion. These are two sides of the same coin. It's about considered reflection, sifting out which parts of socialisation work for us and which don't.

As We Grow Up, We Split

Say you love dancing and perform often and with great joy. Then one day you put on the show of a lifetime for your visiting great-aunt who says you should be ashamed, that proper ladies/ gentlemen would never make such a spectacle of themselves. Ouch! Criticism is experienced as the withdrawal of love. Because children are so sensitive, they feel that loss physically. To stop the pain, to win back the love they feel they have lost, they adjust their behaviour.

Now, if children weren't children, they might be able to say: *Aunt so-and-so is rigid and her comment is meaningless.* But we can't. She is an adult and largely we think adults are speaking the truth. So we take it personally. We take it on board. We believe there is something wrong with us. And we are ashamed.

Right there – we create a gap. Right there is the start of a belief system that is false: *If I express myself, the people I love will reject me.* Over time, if we believe it, we become it. Now if you're lucky, you may be clever enough just to change your behaviour when your great-aunt comes around. But you may doubt yourself so much that you decide that dancing is bad and that, because you love it, you are bad too. And that hurts.

This sort of thing happens over and over again as we are growing up. We do and say things that trigger reactions in others and when they hurt us we stop the flow of our emotion so that we don't feel so intensely. This creates a point of disembodiment.

Think of this wound like a splinter. As long as the splinter is there, we can't use that part of our body normally: instead we develop behaviours that help us avoid it.

Emotionally these are called defences. We change the way we walk to avoid pressing on the sore point. But this has an impact on the whole body, and eventually you put everything else out of alignment. If the splinter stays in long enough, a tough skin develops around it. This is actually very clever – your body does it to protect you. But it means that once you decide to tackle the problem you have to dig your way through a fair bit of build-up.

Emotionally we go through the same process. We need to get back to the source of our patterns. The defence systems can be pretty tough. The deeper and older the wounds, the more dead skin you're going to have to dig through. With every layer closer, you feel more deeply because you are closer to the nerve.

If you're anything like me, you'll find it a clunky process. Moving something that's been an obstacle is a relief – but start using the balls of your feet for the first time in 20 years and you're bound to experience the pain of a twisted hip you didn't even know was there.

Splitting

Why do we split? We do it for many reasons, some of which are listed here:

1. We become who people tell us we are, rather than who we really are;

2. We take on the energies of the people around us because we do not yet know we are separate from them;

3. We model ourselves on adults who themselves are split; and

4. We create blockages.

We Become Who People Tell Us We Are

When we are children, we believe and accept what people tell us about ourselves. Because adults are in a position of authority in relation to us (and need to be) we trust their interpretation of things.

I remember going outside for a drawing class in primary school where we were asked to draw the trees. I drew the trees as I experienced them – full of purple and white energy. I was immensely proud of those drawings. Yet my term school report had straight As except for a D for art. My teacher told my parents that the D had brought down my average and that 'Dionne just doesn't care about art. She doesn't take it seriously.' I could not believe my ears, art was my favourite subject. I was really hurt.

I was used to getting punished for marks below an A and while I waited for the hiding, it never came. That both confused and delighted me. My father, it seemed, did not consider art important either. I took this to mean that art was indeed not important, that I did not take it seriously and that that was okay. From then on, although I never lost my love of art, my abilities were stunted and my drawings remained symbolic and childish. When I finally decided in my late thirties to learn to paint and draw, I would sit at the canvas too scared to make a stroke, afraid that my art teacher would 'fire' me.

Taking on what other people tell us about ourselves happens all the times both positively and negatively. You are wonderful, ungrateful, naughty, good, bad, clever, you don't care about anyone but yourself, you are very confusing, you're really helpful, you're a horrible person. We integrate this emotionally and energetically, and it becomes a part of our understanding about who we are. We respond to people's interpretations of us. That in turn affects how we behave.

We believe what people tell us because we are looking for some way to define ourselves in the world and, as children, we use other people as our point of reference. We look to them for approval. This is very natural and can be used very positively. Watch a child blossom with positive reinforcement.

Becoming whole means starting to identify the inputs we have taken on. We need to clear what blocks us, which can include the 'positive' stuff as well. Think how many people you know who are 'nice' when the best thing they could do for themselves is to say 'no'.

In *Be Your Whole Self*, ask the following questions:

1. What did I learn about myself from others?

2. Is it true?

3. How did it make me behave?

4. What was good about it?

5. Is it something I want to keep, or do I need to re-evaluate?

6. What was damaging about it that I want to change?

7. What is a more accurate reflection of who I really am?

8. What are my values now, specifically?

9. Are there places where my values and behaviours are not aligned?

10. How can I realign them?

As adults we can reject feedback we don't like, but, as kids, we take it to heart. This process is usually innocent on the part of the adult, who is interpreting the world as s/he sees it too. And we all say things in anger or because we are tired, things we don't mean. As conscious adults, we can be careful with this, especially around our own children. And sometimes it's not about what we say at all, but how we are heard.

Of course the other big influence is the society that we grow up in. We learn through unspoken cues what's good and bad. We need rules to live together but each culture has beliefs that can be rigid and damaging for individuals. For example, the way women are valued varies greatly depending on where they live. Some people grow up being diminished because of their colour/religion/ sexuality. Social beliefs can have a profound and lasting impact on our behaviour and must be looked at too. I am not sure we can become self-aware without simultaneously becoming aware of social justice.

Whether you are looking at the people, the culture or the society that affected you, it's important to remember that your healing is a deeply personal process. Especially in our Western confessional culture, too many of us publicise the different awkward stages of becoming who we really are.

There are times when we may need to make things public and address people/society directly, but the majority of the work is to deal with your blocks personally.

I think that being clear as an individual helps any work you do socially or politically because you are coming from the right place and know what's motivating you. Some people process personal anger through causes, and this can be a way of avoiding discomfort even though it's well intended.

We Take On The Energies Of The People Around Us Because We Do Not Yet Know We Are Separate From Them

Why, in our later lives, are we drawn to the kinds of people we knew as kids, even the destructive ones? Because they are familiar. We intuitively understand the way someone with that kind of energy feels and behaves. That's because we grew up around similar behaviours and identify them as normal. For example some people who grew up around violence think it's normal and may not question a violent partner.

Although we have our own patterns, we absorb those of others around us as well. Part of becoming conscious means learning to work out what part is you and what part is someone else, what is coming from the inside and what is coming from the outside? This takes a long time because when we start off most of us are fused, we don't know who we are separate from the energies of those who brought us up. Families (direct or otherwise) are immersed in one big emotional soup.

If our early influences are loving and respectful, we go out into the world with love and respect for others. If you learned that people sort things out by hitting each other, there's a good chance you'll see that as an acceptable way of sorting out your problems. You might not become the bully but you might accept being a victim.

39

No matter. Both are unconscious responses to modelling that disempowers you and neither is healthy.

You are with your parents (or caregivers) day in and day out for the better part of eighteen years. Of course you gravitate to people with similar attributes.

We Model Ourselves On Adults Who Themselves Are Split

We learn to be who we are from people who are themselves split and can only teach us what they know. Our parents/carers are our first and most powerful teachers. They don't need to say anything. We watch, learn and model our behaviour automatically. Did your parents read, write, exercise, go out, sit on the couch, eat properly, gorge fast food, love fruit and vegetables, drink occasionally, binge drink? You probably do too. Modelling is often at the base. What I like about this is that we can always learn new models.

My parents had no idea about how to manage their money. They earned it and spent it. We never owned a house or learned how to save but we went to great restaurants. I went to school with tatty shoes and my toothbrush was replaced once a year, but my father never hesitated to treat a table of twenty people to a meal. There was an issue around spending money on the basics that really counted – a stocked pantry, good basic cosmetics and decent clothes.

I went straight out and repeated that pattern. During college I ate in cafes and filled my cupboards with two-minute noodles. It was only after I had my children that I learned properly how to cook and to allocate money in the weekly budget for buying proper food. I had to consciously remodel my behaviour.

We Create Blockages To Stop Us Experiencing Painful Things

Most of the work in *Be Your Whole Self* is about identifying blocks. Remember that sense of joy you felt running through the garden when you were a kid? You felt it in every cell of your body. Children are just as sensitive to pain. They pull away from it with the same speed at which they remove their hands from a flame. It's a survival technique. Unfortunately, the defences we develop as kids rarely help us as adults.

Imagine you get hit for answering back when you are young. Your survival technique is to keep quiet, which is wise. The body – physical and emotional - does what it has to protect itself. But look at where it gets you as an adult. You certainly can't have a good relationship if you don't speak up about your needs, your feelings and your opinions. You can't have a great job. You can't have equal friendships or a good self-image. As you start becoming whole, you realise that you the behaviours that helped you cope with a certain environment as a child are often the things that stand in your way as an adult. You have to shift those patterns and choose a new way of behaving.

Why We Split

Splitting is necessary and important. It gives us a reason to wake up. Children feel what's going on around them, but they don't yet own their knowledge in a conscious, adult way. This is what the journey is about. Our lives help us become conscious adults and develop specific gifts, gifts I believe are necessary for our life work.

What Does It Feel Like To Be Split?

Everyone has their own particular brand of what it feels like to be split but no matter what your unique experience, it's a bit like having water in your ear – it just doesn't feel right. It makes you uncomfortable in your own skin.

One of my friends, Kate, grew up with an alcoholic father who often flew into violent rages. She watched her mother being beaten up more times that she cares to remember. She used to escape to the backyard to get away. Her father told her that women were useless and she left school early to work. As an adult she married a man who constantly puts her down. She finds herself in holes of self-loathing and is often depressed.

Another friend felt emotionally abandoned when her mother was put into a mental asylum when she was young. All of a sudden she was alone with a father who was under great stress and did not know how to deal with what was going on. As an adult she feels anxious whenever she is alone.

How We Compensate For The Split

We compensate for the deficiencies we feel when we split by developing a mask. We do this because we are afraid that someone will uncover the truth about how insecure and afraid we really are. To do this, we develop personality traits that give us the outcomes we want, including diverting us from those wounds.

Bullies are good examples. Many bullies have been put down and controlled, and are actually very insecure. To compensate for that they need to be right, and they tell themselves that they are right and behave in ways that force others to agree. A challenge brings them face to face with the possibility that they could be wrong and into the pain they have never dealt with. They frighten others into submission. That way they never have to look at why it's so important for them to win. It tends to work and so the mask gets stronger.

Eventually, the bully becomes so closely associated with his or her mask that it becomes impossible to separate the mask from the person. Some bullies are overt. Others are more sophisticated and work passively or through others. This makes the mask even trickier to identify because they recast the mask as 'good'.

Of course the extent to which we are split varies greatly. Some of us might be very obviously depressed or addicted. That's easy to identify – we wake up and don't want to get out of bed. We're thinking about the drink before we get home. We party all night and drag ourselves home, high and late, to avoid being alone.

Others go numb. They have a high pain threshold but they don't feel much joy or love either. They exist, barely. They can't fall in love. Nothing moves them.

Splitting takes many forms. Whatever form it takes, it keeps us from being whole.

Does Being Split Matter?

So does being split impede us in any way? After all, we know that life is not meant to be perfect and we have managed to survive this far, as disconnected as we are.

When we are split, our wounds are in control. When we are split, the patterns we set up to defend ourselves are running the show. If we choose to stay split, then those behaviours will continue to repeat themselves.

I am thinking now about a man I met who was quite conscious. His parents divorced when he was young and he was sent off to boarding school. On the outside he was intelligent, loving, handsome, perceptive and successful but despite all this, his wife cheated on him. His earlier experiences had left him with this belief: *Those I love will abandon me.* He had come to equate emotional abandonment with physical separation and chose to stay with his wife. He was also highly critical of women who worked. As anyone who has been in an empty relationship knows, you can sleep side by side with someone and be in the most devastatingly isolated union. Likewise, you can be separated geographically but close. By criticising working mums, he could experience the brief relief that comes from feeling you are better than others, while avoiding the real dilemma - that his stay-at-home wife was the source of his emotional pain. That abandonment had nothing to do with geography.

Being split matters very much if you do not want to repeat your past.

Why Are We Willing To Put Up With Being Split?

We are willing to put up with being split because we know we can handle it. Sure, our lives aren't great but at least we are alive and not doing too badly. Again, there are people who can handle this. I am not one of them.

Another reason we put up with being split is that when we do stop to go into the pain, we are not sure we can handle it. That is why we need tools that take us forward step by step.

We stay split because we can blame other people for hurting us. Blame takes the pressure off for a time, often long enough to see us through our discomfort.

Sometimes we are not sure the hard work will pay off. And it does take time to shift old patterns, and work.

Last, we are willing to stay split because we want instant results. We think commitment to a lifelong journey means continual pain when really the path is interesting and fun, occasionally difficult but overall joyful.

What Does It Feel Like To Be Whole?

When you are whole, there's continuity between who you are and who you appear to be.

This does not mean you are always happy or do things perfectly. But you are able to be truthful and respect yourself and others.

You have a sense that you belong in this world.

You feel like a real grown-up rather than a frightened kid and even when you feel like a frightened kid, you deal with it.

You don't react wildly to other people's judgements. You are grounded, focussed and know that you have a purpose in the world.

No matter what happens, you have the strength and know-how to accept responsibility for how you behave. Yes, you still make mistakes but you accept that and learn by taking responsibility for them.

You make choices that enable you to be healthy on every level.

You are prepared to work hard to achieve your goals.

You accept and give support freely and live with a sense of gratitude.

Emotion And The Body

The myth that we have to 'rise above' our emotions is especially corrosive to authenticity.

Where is emotion 'kept' such that we imagine we could disentangle ourselves from it?

Emotions are part of the fabric of our bodies. They emerge from internal (biochemical) and external events and in turn trigger internal and external reactions. Their impact is quite simply unavoidable.

The outdated idea (championed by Descartes) that the body and mind can be separated has been sent to the grave by science and its ability to show causality.

While we are still unpacking the complexities of emotions, we know they are both instinctual and cognitive. There's evidence that specific molecules might regulate or, at the very least, be strongly associated with certain emotions, for example, oxytocin with empathy, serotonin with happiness.

The difference in how people deal with emotions is huge. However, we know that emotional intelligence is correlated more strongly with wellbeing and success than IQ. In his work on the social animal, columnist David Brooks believes 'reading and educating your emotions is one of the central activities of wisdom.'

Unfortunately, we have inherited the belief that emotion is inferior to reason. Many psychologies, philosophies and spiritualties demand that emotions be avoided, judged, suppressed.

Out of a genuine desire to be good, many of us have tried to split out the emotional from the other sides of our selves, failing to develop essential skills for dealing with emotional difficulties in the process.

But just because our emotions go unexplored or unexpressed, it does not mean they go away. Quite the opposite, they go underground where they drive behaviours, typically those that undermine us.

Emotional detachment is a defence, a way of avoiding the visceral richness of life.

Although we live in a far more feeling time, in the lust for perfection modern society has a strong preference for the positive over the negative. We're told to be on message, on the money, on the ball. Be positive is practically an anthem.

That's not to say there aren't real benefits to optimism. As I said, living mindfully creates a happiness advantage that helps us cope. But the positive psychology movement of Seligman et al. accepts the link between feeling and functioning: there's no call for denial, just perspective.

But the old split has created a skills deficit. A person who is suffering is told to get over it. Because people don't have the tools to deal with discomfort, theirs or ours, they offer platitudes which, however well-meaning, don't help.

We need techniques that support us to be fully human. The starting point is accepting that all our emotions exist – and are meant to. Anticipation, anxiety, depression, delight, love, loathing – the whole, long list.

We need to allow them all without clinging to any. And to express them without creating further harm.

Often we rush to 'get over' something or 'forgive' someone just to get to the other side. That sort of forgiveness is a decoy, used to divert us from suffering. It's called denial.

It's difficult to stay present when experiencing strong emotions. The body wants to push them away. Our mind doesn't like suffering and thrashes around trying to stop the discomfort now. Enter distraction and addiction. Often we lash out in anger, providing a temporary release but which does not deal with the real problem: pain.

We are scared that if we sit still, we will feel it. And we will. But I put this to you: *We are only feeling what is already there.* Once we allow ourselves to experience it, it lifts. This is the paradox of pain, of avoidance and acceptance.

The Buddhists suggest that we learn to sit in the difficulty and if you've ever practiced it, it's tough. But it sets in train a healing process. We move from understanding we are in the grip of a strong emotion, to accepting the hurt and then knowing that once it has moved through us, we can take appropriate action. Acceptance does not mean being a doormat.

It's okay to feel angry when it's appropriate. If you believe anger is bad and shrug when someone slaps you, then not only do you send the wrong message about how much you value yourself, but the anger also festers.

When we lose something important to us, it's authentic to grieve. No need to get over it, get on with it and get online before the end of the week. Mark the season.

It's important though to distinguish allowing from over-indulgence.

One way to prevent over-identification is to remind yourself that you are not anger, you are just feeling it. It's like looking at your hand and understanding that it's a part of you, but not your totality. I think it's just semantics myself, given that all feelings are temporary, but if it helps then use it.

As you learn that it's safe to feel, you don't fear it any more. You know that whatever you are feeling, it will pass. You lose the need to divide yourself into emotion or reason, good or bad. That makes you authentic and ultimately, imperfectly, whole.

Thinking And Emotion And The Body

No matter how accomplished or 'together' we may appear, we are all facing personal and professional stresses to which none of us has the answer.

And while there is no one way to navigate the overwhelming feelings, we each possess insights or experiences that can help.

Using values as a filter is a practical decision-making tool that creates authenticity.

Why is authenticity important?

Because while the world remains the great unknown that it always was, by making conscious choices (within our constraints), we get to live on our own terms.

That way when things change, as they will, for good or for bad, planned or unexpected, we have an inbuilt sense of meaning.

Having the best available information and by being self-aware (conscious), actively seeking out the new (curious) and applying it to others and ourselves (creative) helps us stay agile and open-minded – key qualities for these times.

So what does being authentic mean?

Clearly there is no one answer, as what is authentic to me might be the antithesis of authenticity to you. More importantly, what was authentic for me at 15 is unlikely to still translate at 30 or 45.

This is a critical insight: who we are is not fixed. Saying 'This is me' in a way that locks us into an invariable idea of who we are or how we should behave can thwart our progress.

Nor is it accurate.

Biologically there's not a cell in your body today that was there when you were born and on average, cells replace themselves every seven years.

Cognitively it's a complex picture.

The way we think remains largely unmapped and therefore the driver for much of what we do is a mystery.

Behavioural theories abound, but the work of Nobel laureate Daniel Kahneman I believe provides golden insights that may constructively influence the way we work and live.

According to him we operate out of two systems.

One is a rapid autopilot that helps us survive but is demonstrably prone to error and very hard to switch off. For example, you see the parallel lines below as of different lengths, even when you know they are equal.

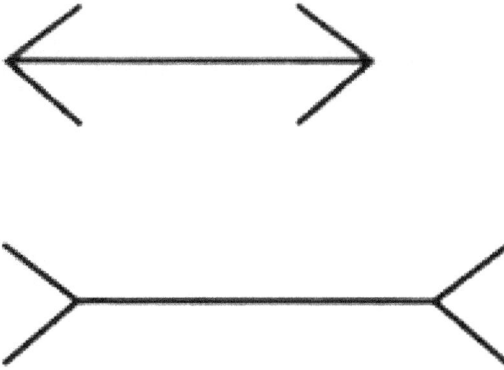

Then there's a more rational side that takes emotion to activate. And given that we are biologically wired to minimise the use of emotion, we don't always flick the switch.

Add this to what we know of the body's preference for retaining the status quo or homeostasis (when you're hot, it cools you down and vice versa) and its social equivalent, system justification bias, and you can see why it is difficult for us to change.

The list goes on. We are anchored by cues of which we are not aware, for example, judges who throw high dice also sentence higher.

Our physical surroundings also influence how we behave.

We are biased towards being <u>optimistic</u> and act differently on the same facts depending on how they are framed. For example, people will opt for surgery with a survival rate of 90% but not with a mortality rate of 10%.

We have little idea of why we do what we do.

This is not to drive home that we are flawed, but to suggest that we accommodate this knowledge by paying attention to it, and slowing down. Look before you leap as our forebears wisely said.

Doing, Being And Values

So given this inconstancy and what appears to be little more than a mosaic with respect to our identity, what makes us 'us'? What creates a cohesive yet flexible self that others recognise and trust?

An answer is *our values*, those qualities that resonate for us personally and reflect on the deepest level what we consider worthwhile.

So my question is - do you know what yours are? If I had to ask you to name your top 20, top 5, top 2, would you readily name integrity over education, pleasure over purity, kindness over self-care, gratitude over charity? We all have a sense of what our values are, but consciously taking the time to define what really drives you takes it to another level.

It's worth taking the time to figure your values out because in an overwhelming world they can be a powerful guiding tool.

You may not know who you are or what you think in any moment, but ultimately, you are defined by what you do.

Whatever we think we are, or say we are, our own and others' perceptions largely result from *what we do*. That is why it is so important to act from our values.

Of course, we are not wholly defined by behaviours nor should we be.

Sometimes life demands we reveal only a sanctioned side of ourselves, such as in an oppressive regime or in unsafe family/ relationships where it is prudent to keep parts tucked away.

Remember that even values cannot be rigidly applied: it is a matter of judgement. This is dangerous territory if used to excuse dishonesty or to trade-off values for inauthenticity, which is not what I am talking about here.

We've probably all been in states at some time or another where we've acted 'out of character'. A normally loving parent may lose their temper, a trusted colleague, unable to hold their ground, might kowtow to a decision they do not like, a partner forget to call the other to advise of a change of plan.

But the very expression suggests that these are anomalous events that do not reflect the way we normally behave. Want to know what truly drives someone? Listen to the words but pay acute attention to the patterns that appear in their lives. These are the shape of accumulated choices, some deliberate, others not, and are a powerful narrative.

It's also important to recognise that how we behave is in part situational.

Emotionally aware people know that different times call for different styles. We may need to be tough in driving a legal outcome but empathetic delivering bad news or responding to someone's pain. This does not lead us away from the core: on the contrary, values act as an anchor from which we extend our reach into the world.

There's a lot of talk about the values-driven life. We hear it when we tell ourselves stories as much as when we tell our story to friends, family, peers.

But what does it mean in tangible ways we can explain and live by?

Would yours be acceptance, assertiveness and authenticity? Compassion, conformity, cooperation? Encouragement, equality, excitement? Or are you about flexibility? Generosity? Honesty and humility? Justice, kindness, order, pleasure, power, reciprocity, respect, self-care, trust? The list is long.

Could you show how these values play out in daily life, where and how you applied them? Would there be a continuum between what you said and did?

It's worth thinking about.

Values are what make us 'us': the parts that cannot be bought or sold.

Say you believe in integrity. Then no matter what the situation you would ask: *How can I behave with integrity in response to this?* You don't look around to see what others consider acceptable and make a decision relative to them: you make it relative to you. If a culture is about the way we do things around here, then the question becomes how I do things within me. That's how you work out if you're aligned with your job or the partnership you're in. It's not, well, everyone does X or Y. It's, I made the decision, I chose.

This is not always easy. All choices bring consequences, including those we refuse to make. There are times when the cost seems too high. Name that too. Mindfulness is a better position to come from.

We are not always aware of the factors that influence decision-making and many sociocultural caveats apply, including where others place the locus of control. Acknowledging differences helps us to claim our space in the world.

Acting from consciousness is what makes us more authentic.

Values are not goals. They are a deep internal drive and ultimately a shaping statement.

And while they therefore cannot be right or wrong, we should keep in mind when applying them as with anything, do no harm. This applies as much to others as ourselves.

Failing to leave an unhappy relationship because a partner will be hurt can be a cop-out if it results in harming ourselves. This does not suggest we should be selfish or bail at the first sign of trouble, but rather be careful not to misuse a so-called value to wriggle out of responsibility because it is difficult.

Likewise this is not about clubbing opinions into others. Saying, 'Your shirt is awful' when no one asks is not honest, just opinionated.

Properly used, values provide a filter that helps us decide what to do and consequently who we become.

Exercise

1. Write a list of your 20 values.

2. Pick your top five. This can be quite hard. Is supporting others more important, for example, than empathy? It can be difficult to distinguish one from the other but that's about getting to the heart of what matters.

3. For at least two of these, write down an occasion where you have lived by that value and where you have not. We've all done this so it is not a matter of berating ourselves for the inconsistency but recognising how easy it is to act in ways that go against the grain.

4. With the benefit of hindsight, how do you believe you could have acted differently? Rewrite the past by preparing a different version of the same event but this time, behaving as you would have liked without fear of retribution or outcomes.

The Be Your Whole Self Process

The essence of *Be Your Whole Self* is simple. It involves two separate but related processes, used over and over again. These processes are:

- Clearing; and

- Nurturing.

Clearing

Wounds create blocks that drive our behaviour. This means we respond to things in predicable ways. It also means we find it difficult to see things in new ways and we apply the same filter, no matter what is happening. For example, 100 good things happen but because we think things always go wrong for us we only remember the one thing that went wrong. As a result, life feels repetitive and we feel stuck.

Blocks suck up the energy. Clearing on the other hand helps you to respond and see things in new ways.

You can always tell when someone is unblocked because they look as if a light has been switched on inside. We all have that light but the intensity depends on the number of blocks we have.

You can see the cycle.

The more wounds you have, the less energy you have; the less energy you have, the less motivated you feel; and the less motivated you feel, the less you do things you love. As a result, you become more and more depleted. On it goes. Before you know it, your life feels dark and meaningless.

Clearing is about becoming aware of what those wounds are and allowing yourself to experience and understand them so that you can transform them.

Nurturing

The more we do things that delight and nurture us, the more we feed our emotional system. The light grows stronger and bubbles up like a fountain. We can also absorb all the wonderful energy around us because we become more open: this fills us up.

For healing to be integrated and enduring, it has to be based as much on feeding ourselves with the good stuff as getting rid of the junk.

Why The Clearing/Nourishing Formula Is So Powerful

Healing in this way is aligned with the most fundamental process of life itself – breathing. You breathe in, you breathe out. The oxygen feeds you and the poisonous carbon dioxide is released. If you breathe in without letting out the old air, you will find yourself gasping. You simply cannot keep going without killing yourself. It is impossible to keep breathing in forever. If you breathe out without sucking in new air, you land up in the same place. These processes cannot and should not be separated. The oxygen and carbon dioxide cycles are just as important as each other. Both are essential to health.

Clearing At All Costs Is A Path To Nowhere

There are techniques that focus on clearing at all costs. They can feel intense because they are cathartic. But often they are temporary. A lot of the self-help rock festivals fall into this category for me.

People start getting in touch with blocked emotions and it's like the big bang. Someone afraid of anger discovers what it feels like to shout and, oh, it's so wonderful, so much baggage released, so quickly. But beware. This kind of healing can be very limited.

There are a number of traps that you can fall into. Some of these are:

1. **You can get stuck in anger**

    Only certain emotions are what I call 'active'. Anger is one of them and that's why anger is so easily targeted in clearing work. And while it is good to get rid of anger, anger is just one of a whole cocktail of emotions. Most of the time if you clear enough anger, you are going to come face to face with the thing that your anger is shielding you from in the first place - your grief.

    Anger is like the outer layer of a wound that peels back to reveal something else lodged deeper in the skin.

    In a sense, anger is the easiest part of the healing process. Once you hit grief – well – that's a different process. Now you need to know how to stay still, to drop down into a place that does not feel so 'active' or 'alive'. That takes another level of courage and unless you have developed your emotional reserve you may not yet have the strength to transition from anger to grief and back out of it.

A lot of people who get addicted to cathartic work stay stuck in anger. Healing for them becomes a cycle of remembering, revisiting and releasing wound after wound. That is the path it offers: *the path of wounds.*

2. **You can create a lot of damage while you are trying to heal**

Another problem with work that encourages you to get it out and express yourself at all costs is that it creates self-help-monsters who often cause more damage trying to get better than they experienced in the first place.

I have been guilty of this myself. I know that when I first went into therapy I almost burst into fire when I got into contact with the depth of my pain and the anger at those who had hurt me (in my mind). I wrote letters and summonsed friends and relatives of all shapes and sizes to give them a piece of my mind. While this took a lot of courage, looking back with what I know now, I would never have done it this way. I hurt some people.

Yes, perhaps what I said to them about what they did and how I felt was true. But the anger was decades old. Only some of it belonged to them. I wasn't aware of the complexities that affected the lives of those who had hurt me. And given I had no compassion for myself, I didn't understand the concept of extending compassion to others for being as flawed as I was.

So often the anger we feel for people only partly belongs to them. There is almost always a deeper, older source. We can find ourselves lashing out at people with a sense of disproportion. Yes, we might need to confront them about their deceit but should they wear the brunt of 35 years of being deceived? That is not right either.

The release we get from working privately is more powerful than taking it out into the public arena.

There are some abuses that need to be exposed publicly, but even so, it's better to get through your own private process first so that you have the strength to go through that very difficult process.

The beauty of private work is that you don't need to censor yourself. You can happily dump fifty years of rage on someone you have known for a year because they will never know about it. A far more complex picture will reveal itself along the way, including some of the choices you have made. This sets a good base for real growth.

3. **Unbalanced healing can be an excuse for avoiding your own shadow**

The other problem with unbalanced clearing work is that we can find ourselves focussing totally on 'the other' person and what they have done to us.

Usually this happens because we have spent a lifetime protecting 'the other' by not speaking out. We have put up with 'the other' or avoided 'the other' or feared 'the other' or denied 'the other'.

We find ourselves saying things like: *you hurt me, you betrayed me, you never loved me, you never cared for me,* and *you always punished me.* It's so all encompassing and dramatic. Although we may feel this way, by doing this we turn ourselves into victims. It becomes about what the world had done to us. Who has hurt us? Who has been so terrible as to deceive us? We are so caught up in our righteous outrage that we don't think about what *we* have done to *us*.

As I have said earlier, blame lifts the lid off the pressure cooker, at least for a while. But where do we go afterwards?

Now that we have pointed our finger, what do we do with the pain, how do we reintegrate it into our bodies? How do we move from seeing ourselves as puppets on which the

71

world has been working out its wrath to active participants in the story of our lives?

Now by that I don't mean we caused the original damage, not at all. But we have certainly made choices around responding to and dealing with it. You need strength if you are to going to be an adult, you need energy and that energy has to come from loving yourself enough to nurture and treat yourself well – every single day.

4. **You're forever preparing the groundwork, getting ready to do something but never doing anything else**

There is of course an obvious question with clearing work, which is: *How are you going to use the emotion that you have freed? What will you put in the hole that you have now cleared?*

It's a bit like gardening, you can spend day after day weeding your yard and this is worthy work. But there has to come a time when you lay down soil and nutrients and then plan what you want to grow. If you just weed the soil without feeding it, there will really be no point. Nurturing encourages you to explore the things that attract you, interest you, which you do well. These give you a sense of meaning.

5. **There are hundreds of clearing/ nurturing tools**

The great thing about *Be Your Whole Self* is that you can use any of hundreds of tools.

That means you can tailor the process to suit yourself. If you don't like one way, try the next. Sooner or later you are going to find the techniques that suit you. I'll tell you some of the processes that work for me:

Clearing:

1. Writing

2. Walking

3. Bathing

4. Breathing exercises

5. Conscious clearing exercises

6. Drinking water

7. Movement

8. Dance

Nurturing:

1. Writing my gratitude list

2. Lighting candles

3. Reading

4. Going to movies

5. Taking time out

6. Dinner with friends

7. Dinner with myself

8. Cooking a special meal

9. Baking

10. Walking near water

11. Doing yoga

12. Going to concerts

The list goes on and on.

It's important to identify what works for you and what you enjoy because that is something you are going to want to keep up.

For me, writing for half an hour each morning is not a task, it's a delight. Bathing by candlelight is not exactly stressful either. I want you to realise that although the process of clearing and nurturing takes you into different emotions, the process is also fun.

The Wholeness Cycle

Now that we've looked at clearing and nurturing in general terms, it's important to spell out some of the milestones.

Part 1

When you first start *Be Your Whole Self*, you will feel better than you have in a while. That's because you are doing something good for yourself and your body responds with joy. You feel uplifted, excited, hopeful that this time it will really work.

You shift perspective and start to make deeper connections with yourself. That's really nice too. It's like: *Oh, I didn't realise I liked red so much, isn't that interesting? So why do I always wear blue?* It's like catching up with a long-lost pal. *Where have you been? What have you done? It's so great to meet you again.* And feeling good makes it easy to stay on track.

Part 2

Once you have some energy reserves, you'll find a block comes up that you need to clear. You don't need to worry about mapping out which issues you want to work on or when. Life has a way of bringing up something.

Whatever has come up is going to trigger some emotion. Say you find yourself dealing with a bully boss and you might feel anxious. If your partner is being lazy and you might feel angry or used.

Whatever the specific emotion, it will likely make you feel uncomfortable. Here is where the challenge begins.

Since we are consciously working to become integrated, we have an opportunity to deal with the emotion differently.

First of all, instead of groaning about it (*Oh no, here it comes again*) we can stop and say: *Well, here it is, my first opportunity to do some real work about transforming this block. I am* (insert authentic emotion eg. nervous) *but I know that it's come up because my body feels supported enough to handle it.*

Bang, right there, you have shifted your perspective and that alone will trigger change. Right there you have stopped yourself from going onto autopilot. Usually when we feel bad, we reach for alcohol or food or work or our addiction of choice to distract us. Now we will try to stay with the discomfort until it works its way through and out of us, noticing the thoughts that are triggered and the emotions and events that come up.

As you do this, the energy that is tangled up in these very emotional memories or experiences has a way of firstly making you feel the discomfort more deeply but then once you sit through it, lifting it up and out of you.

You will feel more deeply inside yourself and also lighter. And just like that, you will start to feel better than you did before.

The Cycle Over Time

Now imagine this cycle, day in and day out, week in and week out, and so forth, year after year.

The start is going to be harder because you have a lot more blocks to clear and less practice at doing so.

There are shorter distances between the cycles of clearing and growth. You have a couple of great weeks, then you start to feel wobbly. You get through that and you have a couple of great weeks again and then, oh no. You may feel like you are on a seesaw.

Some people say they feel worse because they've gone from feeling numb most of the time to feeling a combination of emotions.

But over time as blocks clear, the distance between the cycles gets longer and the depth at which you experience your emotion becomes deeper and more intense.

You may have four great weeks before you hit a wobbly, or eight, or twelve. You could spend whole tracts of your year just living with a sense of wellbeing (which is not the same as happiness).

It takes time to realign your whole self to the way it should be. There's no set pattern. Your body will decide the order of what needs to be done. Your job is to honour its wisdom and your personal path.

Sometimes as you drop down, it is not about clearing wounds anymore, it is about going into unchartered territory. You get beyond the levels of consciousness you know and expand.

Clearing

Stocktake

We are going to start with a personal stocktake. This is where I ask you to take a good, honest look at your life. What is going on around you right now? How do you feel about it? What do you like? What do you want to change?

In order to move forward, you need to know where you are. If you think of this as a journey, then what you are doing is putting a mark on the map. Marking out 'I am here' allows you to define the path you need to take to forge ahead.

So why are we so afraid of being honest about where we are at? Why don't we just own up to what's going on in our lives? Why do we duck and weave around our truth instead of calling a spade a spade and working from solid ground? There are many reasons.

Denial

Quite frankly, sometimes we can't be honest with other people because we don't know how to be honest with ourselves. We don't even know what our 'self' is. We don't remember what s/he likes or wants because it has been a long time since s/he saw the light of day.

We've become used to liking things because other people approve of them. We want things that we think will get us love rather than what really fills us up. We so desperately want external approval

81

that we are prepared to become chameleons in order to fit in. We are so used to being on autopilot we don't know there is another way to be.

Denial Helps To Keep Our Mask In Place

Remember, your defences are there for a reason. They keep your wounds hidden and protect you. The way you behave comes from this space. Your behaviours form your personality, the face you show to the world and by which people define you. If you've made it this far, like all of us you'll have some pretty sophisticated masks in place. By now you probably even like them. Even if you don't, you'll be invested in keeping them because they are a shield between you and your pain.

Let's say that you are a businessperson and a lot of people rely on you to be in control and authoritative, and you've always been that way. But on the home front, your relationship is suffering. Yet no matter how many times people ask how you are, your answer is always the same – great. Other people have problems but you've got it all worked out. People tell you how amazing you are, how strong, how resilient. That feels pretty good. So now you're invested in keeping the image.

Now I am not saying that you should bare your soul inappropriately. There is nothing worse than having a practical stranger spill the contents of their personal life and it's a sure sign that the person is not doing any internal processing. But when a close friend asks you and you give the same answer? Or worse, you tell yourself in the face of turmoil that everything is still fine.

Why do we do that? It's simple. As soon as we acknowledge that things may not be so good, we have to deal with a reality outside the frame we use to define ourselves. And that impacts on the way other people see us as well. Perhaps we would lose their respect. No longer are we the strong one who can cope with everything. We'd have to put up with being imperfect and vulnerable like everyone else. What a shame. That makes us just a little bit shaky. We've become attached to having the outside world say we are worthwhile and if we've found a way to get that, we are going to want to keep it up. The risk seems too high. So rather than redefine who we are and broaden our scope, we redefine the situation instead.

But I will let you in on a little secret, even though deep down you probably already know it. We are all human and there is stuff going on under the surface, no matter how intact the mask. Every person I have ever met is imperfect and vulnerable. I am, you are. Some of us can pretend better than others - that is all. But it is still only pretence. We go to huge lengths to present ourselves as somehow immune from emotion as if that makes us more advanced than other people. This is ridiculous. It is impossible to go through life without being impacted – that is what life is for. Whether it's pleasure or pain, we only know we are alive because we respond with our senses to the things around us. And do you know something else – the only people who buy your pretences are those who are as invested in them as you are. Usually it's because they are trying to get away with the same thing.

Watch a group of people together and you will see this in action. Check out some private school mums after school drop-offs at a local café – the rules might be about money and looks. The game is exclusion/inclusion – who is in and who is out. Whoever is out is judged as different, not good enough, not 'one of us'. But they are no different from hard-core left- or right-wingers where the entry ticket is shared political passion and disdain for the other side. Same game.

Hardliners on a construction site might be earning six figure salaries but the story will still be about 'us and them', the workers and the managers. And it works just as well the other way round, professionals who respect the trades less for no other reason than it makes them feel better. We are hell-bent on playing this 'you are in and you are out' game.

We love it because once we find a place where we are in, we feel more secure. Most of us need to make other people wrong to make ourselves right. We need to put others down to put ourselves up. But I will tell you now that we can never be free when our self-worth depends on an external yardstick.

You have to get to the point where you like who you are, regardless of what anyone else thinks. Whether someone says you are great or horrible should make no difference. The source of your self-love should be yourself.

What any group has in common is that they help each other to prop up the shared false beliefs of what it means to be included in that particular group, *separate from and better than something else.* The detail of the mask is different but the intention is the same – to join together and assert this is the right way to be.

But we know deep down that it's not the full story. What you really have here is a kind of mutual agreement to keep what you know about each other's game under wraps. That is all. You all know that you know. So you see, even then the secret is out.

Denial Is Painful But It Keeps Us Out Of A Much Deeper Pain

Denial is painful but it keeps us out of a much deeper pain, which is why it's so useful. The pain is who we think we are without a mask to protect us.

If you've had a hard life and pride yourself on being tough then you'll judge emotional people as weak. You learned that to survive you could not afford to feel deeply so you named deep feelings as weak and weak as bad in your books. So you criticise emotional people – they are weak but you are strong - they are different from you. You need this to identify yourself as different. Feeling becomes the yardstick. This only reinforces your mask because now you've really got to keep your feelings suppressed or you'll land up on the pointy end of your own finger.

But on a deep level you know that all people feel deeply. And if you stopped to really think about this then you would be forced to conclude that either all humans are weak, or that feeling deeply is not wrong. Either conclusion would challenge your firmly-held belief in your own rightness – in your very definition of self. So you decide, quite unconsciously, that you are willing to pay the price for denial. Sure, you suppress your emotions and suspect that some of the things you're riding on are fake and even that some people see through them, but because you can get away with it most of the time, it's a much smaller price to pay than unravelling.

When I was at university I was really invested in my image as a modern, urbane intellectual. Although I had always been spiritually inclined, I hid this part of myself out of embarrassment that it was not cool enough and worse, I mocked people who were open about their spirituality. Now anyone with a shred of insight would have challenged me on why this issue triggered me so much, but people were too terrified because I had a well-honed tongue and generally took no prisoners. The fact is that my whole life has been a quest for understanding.

My earliest dilemmas were around paradoxes like the existence of bad in a context of absolute good. As a child I was fascinated by religion and philosophy. But I was hurt. I felt let down, abandoned, unable to cope. I decided that a God who was kind would not have exposed a child to my life and therefore could not exist. That was an easier decision for me than my deeper suspicion, lodged in low self-worth, that if God existed then s/he must really have hated me and singled me out for payback. This was a child's way of thinking. Both conclusions were excruciating so rather than look at my false logic I took the easier path – I attacked anyone who raised the mirror. I named spiritually open people as 'wrong'.

Later, when I started to embody spirituality, I had to drop the mask around this. I knew I would be on the receiving end of judgements just like mine. That was painful. It was like coming out of the closet and it took a lot of courage.

Naturally what happened as I shifted my perspective was that I started to judge those who were open spiritually as right. I went the other way. This is the reformed smoker syndrome in action. I couldn't believe how closed cynics were.

It took many years for me to drop my attachments to either of those views and to settle into my own understanding of the world without reference to other people's yardsticks.

Now really, it's irrelevant whether or not you believe in a higher power. What matters is what is driving your judgements of yourself and others.

Denial Gives Us A Valid Reason To Keep Stalling

Denial gives us a good reason to keep stalling instead of moving into action. If we can't really see the detail of how bad things are, then we can tell ourselves things aren't actually that bad and we don't have to make any difficult new decisions. We can just stay right where we are.

Self-Sabotage

So why do we often make choices that take us away from what we want rather than towards it?

We say we want something, then do everything in our power to ensure we don't get it.

Either we're lying to ourselves about what we really want, in which case we need to do a bit of soul searching, or else we need to work out why we behave so destructively.

A while ago I was at a dinner with a friend and her wonderful partner. She genuinely wanted a great relationship, yet she'd invited an ex-lover to the occasion with whom things were still unresolved. You can imagine how that played out. While she relished the attention, her partner gradually withdrew. He may not even have known why. She sensed that and in turn became defensive. By the end of the night, everyone was unhappy.

Why did she do that? On the one hand, she wanted to be central and feel safe in a relationship, yet she had put her partner in a situation where he was not.

Self-sabotage can be more subtle. We want a better relationship with our kids but end up staying late at work and missing important events. We let those closest to us down by failing to make them a priority.

It's not just in relationships that we undermine our goals.

We have an important presentation to prepare but distract ourselves with minor activities with the end result that the presentation does not deliver on expectations. We might long for a home but fritter money on shoes rather than saving for a deposit. Or say we want to slim down but accept another glass of wine.

The roots of self-sabotage are complex. As Dr Laurie Santos' monkey experiments suggest, irrationality could be embedded in our evolution, which might make it more difficult to conquer, but no less necessary.

Sometimes we don't think we are worthy of having what we want. This is the result of low self-esteem and is rarely apparent on the surface, with many self-destructive people appearing confident. Our saboteurs lurk below the surface of consciousness, waiting to pounce.

As to why we suffer from low self-esteem, there are hundreds of books on the subject.

People who are treated poorly suffer terribly from self-doubt. They believe they are as they are treated. This is one of the most powerful and destructive myths and can set up cycles of abuse over generations.

Children believe what adults tell them because they trust them and have to in order to survive. That's a compelling motivator for morphing into other people's ideas of who we are, but if we continue behaving that way, we never leave home in the emotional sense. Now that we are adults we also know firsthand how full of nonsense we can be. We need to apply that recognition backwards through time.

But it's not all upbringings. As psychologist and professor emeritus of Stanford University Philip Zimbardo's infamous prison experiments show, even healthy adults who are forced to live in destructive environments suffer breakdowns. We are not our environments and yet we can become what our environment tells us we are. That makes the work of identifying triggers critical.

Some people habitually repeat behaviours that once got them an outcome they liked with little regard for consequences. They act on autopilot: it was a fling, it's just who I am, it meant nothing to me. And yet it meant so much to those it hurt.

These people are asleep. Their craving for short-term gratification outweighs everything else. They may point the finger at gamblers or alcoholics but they are no less addicts.

Others use their strengths but cannot adapt. A hard-nosed negotiator with a winner-takes-all approach might succeed in some situations but fails to build long-term relationships at work or at home.

People also over-identify with who they believe they are and cannot contextualise. Although an extreme example, a boisterous person might act like that at all times, even say at a funeral, because they argue 'that's just me'. Emotionally this shows a lack of intelligence, even if they are smart in other ways.

The self is not stone: philosopher Julian Baggini reminds us that there is not a cell in us today that was there when we were born and our memories are scientifically proven to be fallible. The self becomes what we decide it is. This is what makes it possible to bring our aspirations and our actions together.

So how do we do that? How do we get out of the way and stop sabotaging our dreams?

First we have to become aware of what we are doing and why. Anthony De Mello is to the point – 'What you are aware of you are in control of; what you are not aware of is in control of you.' Later I discuss how naming the game can help.

But that's not always easy. Lots of people don't want to do the hard work of waking up, they're happy sleepwalking: I vote X because my father/mother did, as did their parents and theirs and my great-greats before that. And there's our identity – decided four generations ago without any input on our part. I am not sure we should brag about it.

Awareness can be difficult. It brings us face to face with the harsh reality that we are the only ones who can change. We have to accept that other people are who they are. How frustrating! We'd be happier if they just did as they were told.

In fact, this knowledge is liberating because it means we don't have to stick around waiting. We look at them and say: That's who they are: I accept it. It doesn't mean we like them or stay in situations that are bad for us or fail to protect ourselves from the consequences of their actions. It doesn't mean we don't challenge existing laws or try to rectify social injustice. It's the opposite. By accepting things as they are, we recognise we are the ones who will have to do the hard work – and so we do – either by changing the situation or our reaction to it.

While identifying our destructive tendencies is imperative, it's often not enough to stop us flying off the handle. We are programmed to run in a certain way.

We need techniques that translate awareness into meaningful action. Insights are not enough. We already have a hundred insights, a thousand. We are so overwhelmed with insights that we are paralysed into inaction.

And we're busy people. We're juggling partners, kids, work, health and finances as well as pursuing nobler dreams in the moments we have spare. There's enough to do. No more insights, we need outcomes.

What we have to do is create a gap between any trigger and our pre-programmed response to it. We need to do something that will stop us in our tracks and give us enough time to remix – to make a conscious choice instead of a predictable one.

Here's a simple but powerful suggestion: *slow down*.

'I say potato, you ...' – take a deep breath, step away from yourself and be aware that the unconscious puppet master has arrived. Ask: *What is really happening here?*

Sit down, shut up and do not step into the emotional minefield. Instead see clearly, accept the situation as it is (rather than as you would like it to be) and take time out to synthesise before you act (this is, of course, unless decisive action is needed).

This technique, applied over and over again, mindfully rather than by rote, will stop you blowing yourself and others up. Over time it builds an authentic, rather than an unconscious, platform.

Can you adopt this as a mantra and use it to inform you in the same way as your authentic guiding principle determines how you use your time?

Slow down before you invite your ex to the party. Do you really want a great relationship? Will doing this create a strong foundation, or undermine it? Don't be so worried about giving something up. Put your emotions into the current wo/man and if it doesn't work out, that's when you can open your options up.

Slow down before you hand over your credit card for a fourth pair of black shoes. Do you really need them? Can you wait another week before you decide? Challenge yourself to wear the other three pairs first.

Slow down before you refill that glass. Have some water instead. Tell yourself that if you still want another wine in half an hour that you will have one then. Buy yourself time.

It's not as easy as it sounds, slowing down in the heat of the moment. But it will help you to stop kicking yourself in the teeth and get you to use your feet to do better things – like taking one more step in the right direction.

Name The Game

If you want clarity, you're going to need to strip to the bare bones. The most popular strategy people use to wiggle out of responsibility and make you feel bad is the blame game.

This is what normal people do. You make a mistake at work. You go straight to your boss and say: You need to know I've stuffed up and this is how I am trying to fix it. S/he knows the lay of the land and your emotions can be used to find a solution instead of turning in on you as anxiety. Herein ends the need for the Inquisition.

Isn't that great? You're human. You made a mistake. You acknowledge it and get on with it. Accountability creates clarity and you'd think everyone would want that but sadly, this is not always the way. Many prefer to dodge consequences and point the finger.

There are numerous reasons why we do this.

When we do something wrong, we feel bad. We don't like that. The tension between what we think and do is called <u>cognitive dissonance,</u> a sort of mental pressure that is released if we can close the gap. Often this involves mental gymnastics.

We smoke, knowing it's poisonous, so we tell ourselves it's a way to manage stress. Or we cheat on our partner but tell ourselves the relationship was already falling apart. Lash out, but say we were provoked into doing it. Self-justifications may be irrational but because they help us avoid pain, we use them.

It would be easier if we could just accept that pain is inevitable. Buddhists believe we should neither deny nor exaggerate pain, and we should practice what's called Zazen to balance the autonomic nervous system by sitting in the discomfort – if you can – until it passes.

However some others have no interest in playing it straight and enjoy the negativity generated by lashing out. Their outbursts are like an electric charge, filling them with excitement. Drama makes them feel alive. Let me show you how it works.

You approach an employee to ask about a deadline they've missed. They launch into a tirade about how unrealistic their workload is and how incompetent their colleagues are, and then throw in for good measure, 'By the way, don't let on I told you this but watch your back, I hear so and so has it in for you.'

You leave shaken, confused and without a revised deadline.

Not only have they managed to divert you from the original issue but also you are destabilised. You might even believe they are an ally looking after your back.

The beauty of this particular attack is that it is disguised as support. Blamers are fantastic at diversionary tactics. There are many subtleties to their approach but see if you can spot the theme.

You tell your partner that you're upset that s/he secretly had dinner with an ex and s/he shakes her/his head in disbelief, disappointed that 'You've really got a problem with other wo/men'.

This leaves you feeling inadequate and shameful for being so distrusting.

Notice what is happening.

These fast talkers, proficient at emotional volleyball, say something that takes your focus off the real issue and places it on something else – from the missed deadline to the workplace subterfuge, from the ex-lover to your insecurity. Slam!

Worse, they deliver the message in way that makes you question yourself. You go in to resolve a problem but leave believing you are the problem instead. Before you know it, you lie dazed on the floor, wondering where the rug has disappeared to.

The other thing about blamers is that they like getting others involved. Whether it's involving you in 'innocent' gossip or something more sinister, they love accomplices. That way when the game is named, they can point the finger and say, 'You did it too'. 'If you tell A what I said about B then I will tell B what you said about him.' Collusion is their modus operandi, their protection.

These hunter-gatherers appear first as allies, building trust and an inventory before they start winding you in. That is how you become a shield. There's the cheater who persuades a faithful friend to join a dating site, then shares stories of exploits with their 'like-minded' friend, ensuring neither betrays the other. Your defence is not to become involved.

Although they come in all shapes and sizes, there are some things blamers have in common.

Words are their weapons. No matter how many you have, they have more. You can never beat them at this game. They love the thrill of spinning a web so complex you do not even realise you are caught. Negativity is delicious to them.

If you lift the covers, interactions will usually show the following: whatever they are saying/doing, it is something that will help them get their own way, no matter who has to pay. The best of them do so in a way in which they don't even appear to be selfish, 'I am only doing this for you.'

So how do we deal with these kinds of people?

To stop them, you need to slow down. This gives you time to consciously recognise what is happening and get the conversation back on track.

Imagine the scenario above. Your colleague goes off, you:

1. Name the game. Say to yourself, 'I am dealing with a blamer'. This will allow you to anticipate what is coming.

2. Name the game plan. You know a blamer is going to try and draw you away from the real issue. Say it in your mind. This person is going to try and divert me from the real issue. Only the tactics will change. Sit back and try to spot them. Mark each new approach on an imaginary scorecard: 1 – blames workload, 2 – tries to undermine colleagues, 3 – tries to make themselves an ally/insider.

3. Listen. Don't respond. Most of the time they will interrupt you anyway. They like to control the conversation from start to finish, often practicing it in their minds beforehand. They cannot adapt to the unexpected and have to cut you off to stay in control. If this happens, just stop.

4. Understand (for yourself) what they are avoiding. They are afraid there will be a consequence for not delivering the report on time.

5. State what you need clearly, 'That's not the issue. I need to know when I can realistically expect that report. Let's set up a time to work through your workload. In the meantime, what's your revised deadline?'

Do not buy in.

And if s/he's a cheater, recognise and accept them for that. You can't change them, you can only change your reaction. Recognise the harm they are doing to you if you allow it to continue, and consider honestly if you should leave the relationship.

Nurturing

Setting Goals

By now we understand a little bit more about our biology and biases and how they influence our behaviour. We need to set some goals for where we want to be.

Like knowing our values, setting goals can be a useful way to direct energy. There are only so many hours in each day so knowing we will do X instead of Y, because X is aligned with where we want to go and Y is not, is useful.

Knowing what we truly value cuts through the <u>excesses of choice</u> (and resultant emptiness) and steers us in the right direction.

I would like to dispel some outdated beliefs about goals and motivation that are useful to know, including that money alone motivates us to perform.

While a lack of money certainly contributes towards unhappiness, studies consistently show that above a certain number ($75,000 by the <u>Princeton studies</u>), it makes no difference at all.

Commentators like <u>Daniel Pink</u> argue counter-intuitively that while money can motivate those doing formulaic tasks with predictable outcomes, it has little influence on those whose work is creative or demands the kind of collaborative and complex thinking required in today's world. Worse, it can displace intrinsic motivation. We seek meaning. That is a reality and it is most often found in creating good relationships (with ourselves and others) and purposeful work.

Some people, like author <u>Daniel Markovich</u>, argue that setting stretch goals can sap you of motivation and that small but achievable wins will take you forward step by step, while others, like <u>Steve Denning</u>, believe big and small goals can coexist.

You will need to work out what works for you. Personally, I like to keep stretch goals in mind while focussing on little milestones that remind me that I am on course.

Either way, we know that taking action has a positive impact on behaviour. This is borne out by the psychological research – the <u>Zeigarnik effect</u> shows that anything that triggers action moves us forward, lodging the goal in our minds.

It's also useful to know that when you set a short-term goal to give something up, you become prone to the what-the-hell effect, as any dieter by Monday midday has experienced.

If you want to avoid the had-a-chocolate-so-might-as-well-have-fries-with-that-and-yes-do-upsize-the-Coke mindset, then set long-term goals in which you acquire something rather than giving something up.

Go ahead and list the goals that you want to achieve.

Committing To Kindness

I am a great believer in practicing kindness to oneself and others.

And while we are supposedly more open to softness and emotion, the reality is that we still privilege disconnection. By this I mean that the hard-nosed, cut off and detached person can be perceived as more capable and grown-up than their more sensitive peers.

Although they rarely are more capable and grown-up or, in fact, even hard-nosed, the image is revered and therefore reinforced.

But it's a myth. Underneath, as I have already said several times, we are all vulnerable.

This doesn't mean we can't manage emotions appropriately or make difficult decisions. We navigate these complexities daily.

In fact studies show that survivors of abuse <u>accept</u> vulnerability as a way to build strength and authenticity.

But hardness? Hardness is a defence and it should not be confused with courage any more than someone who avoids dealing with real problems because they are difficult should be labelled kind.

Kindness takes courage.

Of course it's easy to be kind when we're in a great space and the world is working with us but when times are tough or we're under stress it is a greater challenge.

It's so much easier to lash out than it is to take a breath and deal with our own frustration.

And while doing so releases the pressure valve in the short term, you have to ask yourself what you are creating in the longer term and if that is what you really want.

Do you want a productive, trusting relationship with your colleagues? A connected, loving relationship with your partner or child? Will lashing out really help you accomplish that, or will it build walls?

I'll bet that kindness (which includes being able to disagree, be firm or tackle difficulty) is better at creating long-term good.

And yet it doesn't always seem to work like that.

We hear of ruthless managers surrounded by people only too willing to do their bidding and many climb the corporate ladder where there are seemingly no consequences for the way that they act.

But are these people following them out of respect for their ability or character? No, it's just fear.

To excuse a lack of empathy, some people retreat to evolution, talking about survival of the fittest as if it precludes kindness.

But survival of the fittest does not mean dog-eat-dog.

Darwin has been greatly misinterpreted.

Director of the Berkeley Social Interaction Lab, Dacher Keltner, says Darwin believed sympathy was a stronger instinct than self-preservation and that we are profoundly cooperative in the way we live.

So why does the message get lost? Why are kind people sometimes seen as soft? Why is emotional sensitivity confused with weakness?

For a long time people thought it was possible to separate reason from feeling and that the job of the mind was to keep emotion under control.

This stemmed from the belief that body and mind were separate, something science has shown to be false.

The body and mind are so intimately connected that even the way we move impacts our thoughts and actions and vice versa.

And what we know is that being kind is not just good for us emotionally but physiologically too.

When we support others we increase the <u>dopamine</u> in our brains, giving us a kind of high. Emotional warmth also produces <u>oxytocin</u>, which reduces blood pressure and the free radicals and inflammation associated with ageing.

But the best thing is that kindness is contagious.

A <u>recent</u> study showed an <u>anonymous</u> person who donated a kidney set off a ripple where others did the same until thirty people received a new kidney as a result of that one act of kindness.

And the finding has been <u>replicated</u>.

In a game where selfishness made more sense than cooperation, acts of kindness still tripled over the course of an experiment by other subjects who were influenced to contribute more.

But it is a case of monkey-see, monkey-do, which means that selfish behaviour can also be replicated.

That makes it important not just to role model the behaviour you'd like to see but to choose wisely who you keep around.

So if you find yourself being seduced by the aura of a can-do boss who takes no prisoners, or are on the verge of lashing out at your friend, stop and consider this.

The cost of unkindness to yourself and others is huge.

And it's not just body and soul, it has a domino effect on the world.

Three tips:

1. Do one kind thing for yourself each day that does not involve buying something.

2. Do one kind thing for someone else.

3. And if you are yourself on the verge of being unkind, stop and reflect. What is your long-term goal? And how will what you are about to do help you accomplish that? Slow down, slow down, and slow down.

The Be Your Whole Self Practice

When I was putting *Be Your Whole Self* together, I tried to focus on only those tasks that would have the biggest impact on shifting emotional patterns. That is because I know you are busy and life is complex enough as it is.

If you do nothing other than the tasks below, then I feel sure that they alone will assist you to live a happier and more fulfilling life.

Your Weekly Cleansing Bath (Clearing)

Put 500g of bicarbonate of soda and 500g of rock salt in a bath and bath for 30 minutes. When you are finished, shower off and wash your hair.

Going out into the world is like leaving home dressed in a white suit – no matter how careful you are, by the end of the day you'll have tell-tale signs of dirt. Emotionally it's the same. The cut and thrust of everyday life builds up emotionally and physically. This bath is a powerful way to release pent-up stress.

I do this bath at least once a week, sometimes twice if I am particularly stressed or dealing with difficult issues.

I have given this recipe to so many people over the years and they all report an instant sense of being lighter, freer and clearer.

If you don't have a bath then be inventive. I had a big plastic toy box in the shower for a year at one of my homes. Each week I would fill it up and squish myself into it, although I was only able to either dunk my chest and torso or my legs and torso in at any one time. At the end of my bath I would have to tip out the water and get the box cleaned and out before I could shower.

For a few years before that, when my shower was too small for even a toy box, I just used to sit on the couch with my feet soaking in a salt-bicarbonate bucket. Do what you can do.

The key for this half an hour a week is: *quiet, solitude and reflection.*

Also the combination of hot water and the salts can make your heart beat faster so, health first always, be careful. Ensure it is right for you.

Your Daily Gratitude List (Nurturing)

I've always practiced conscious gratitude and while there are writers who have focussed on this as their life's work, you'll also find the idea central to many emotional and spiritual doctrines.

As part of your practice, write down five things that you are grateful for each night.

Focussing on what you have rather than what you don't have, and on all the goodness in your life, creates a dramatic change in your perception. You move from feeling victimised to acknowledging just how much you have and how richly you are supported by life.

So every night before you go to sleep write down five things for which you are grateful. They can be small or big – whatever springs to mind.

1. I am grateful I got that submission finished at work today. It's been hanging over me.

2. I am grateful I had to deal with Dan's aggression at work today because it showed me that I don't have the tools I need to handle him and I need to find out what I can do to get them.

3. I am grateful for my kids.

4. I am grateful for this electricity bill because even though it made me wince I know it allows me to have hot showers and I really love them.

5. I am grateful I can see, hear, walk and think.

By focussing on what is wrong, we ignore the many blessings of our daily lives. Some people would gladly work their entire lives if it were possible to buy some of the things we take for granted - like eyesight. Gratitude creates appreciation and a sense of worth and well-being.

Gratitude helps you to open your eyes to what you have rather than what you don't. This change in perspective, although wonderful all on its own, will help you later on to see your blocks as gifts rather than obstacles.

One Act Of Self-Nurturing Every Day (Nurturing)

This is a nurturing tool that will build up your energy and allow you to do powerful clearing work.

Your task is to ensure that you do one thing that nurtures you each day. What that is, is up to you.

A short walk.

A special food treat that you don't allow yourself very often.

New socks.

A home cooked meal.

Fresh flowers for your bedside.

A matinee with a good friend.

A day off work.

Try to stay away from buying things as a treat only because it reinforces that it's all about having money, which it is not.

In order to get the most out of clearing, you need to have enough energy to take you all the way through a cycle – from end to end – to ensure that you don't get stuck halfway.

Mindful Engagement (Clearing And Nurturing)

Be mindful.

Recognise when you are in denial and why, and think about how you can handle the situation differently.

Slow down before making choices.

Create clarity by naming what you are dealing with.

Practice Kindness

Do one kind thing for yourself and one for others every day.

Resources

Given my passion for understanding the science behind <u>behaviour and bias</u> I recommend highly:

1. The _Antidote: Happiness for people who can't stand positive thinking_ by Oliver Burkeman. That's me - I find positive thinking too superficial.

2. _Brain Rules_: 12 Principles for Surviving and Thriving at Work, Home and School by Dr John Medina.

3. _The Emotional Life of Your Brain_ by Dr Richard Davidson and Sharon Begley.

4. _The Brain that Changes Itself_ by Dr Norman Doidge

5. _Women Who Run with The Wolves_ by Clarissa Pinkola-Estes

6. _Toxic Parents_ by Dr Susan Forward. This has a confronting title, but even if you have great parents, this book is worth reading for understanding emotional patterns.

About The Author

Photograph: ericalgara.com.au

Dionne Kasian-Lew is a respected thought leader, professional speaker and published author.

A blogger at The Connected Leader blog and Be Your Whole Self, her writing is influenced by a lifelong love of art, science, quantum physics, psychology, philosophy, theology and endless curiosity about human behaviour.

Dionne is a qualified coach and mentor, committed to supporting her clients to achieve their highest potential.

In addition to being a social leadership consultant and corporate affairs expert, Dionne is a painter who has had several exhibitions of her work.

Connect with her at:

Web: beyourwholeself.com

Twitter: @beyourwholeself

Email: dionne@dionnekasianlew.com

www.ingramcontent.com/pod-product-compliance
Lightning Source LLC
Chambersburg PA
CBHW020506030426
42337CB00011B/251